DEATH RATTLE

EQUITY LOST Included

S. E. McKenzie

S. E. MCKENZIE

DEATH RATTLE: Equity Lost included

DEDICATION
To everyone who has been left out in the cold.

S. E. MCKENZIE

This book is a book of speculative fiction. Characters, companies, governments, places, events, are either products of the author's imagination or used fictitiously. Any resemblance to persons (living or dead), companies, governments, places and/or events, is a coincidence.

DEATH RATTLE: Equity Lost included

TABLE OF CONTENTS

S. E. MCKENZIE

DEATH RATTLE

DEATH RATTLE

I

How brave were we;
Never questioned those above;
Steely eyed;

Now lying in this field;
With no color at all;
For this was last call.

The battle cry
We heard
Moved us

Like a herd
Too fierce
To be called sheep

Now so many lie here
Gasping for breath
While drowning in death.

We are just living cells;
Dying one by one;
Dying before life has really begun.

S. E. MCKENZIE

Our side has a Holy Book
Their side has a Holy Book
And we had no time to look

Inside either book
For ourselves
And now we never will.

II

So ready were we for battle;
But nothing prepared us well
For the Death Rattle Hell.

We heard each other's chilling Rattle all around;
As we were lying on the ground.
We expected Heaven's Door

To open; and nothing more.

Our eyes were focused on the sky
And wondered why all we could hear
Was each other's after battle Death Rattle.

We stared at the sky anyway
While the birds flew all around
Their song could not drown

DEATH RATTLE: Equity Lost included

Death Rattle's chilling sound.
There was no Angel's Welcome
Though it might yet come.

We heard
Trumpets blaring
But they were only our own.

We had thirst but could not drink
We were drowning in death
And struggling for breath.

It was hard to say what we missed the most
As we were becoming part of our Living Host.
We could not tell the fully living

What they needed to know; what we know now;
If we had only been more loving and giving
We would have all reached a higher standard of living.

It was not too late for the fully living below;
To change the Mastermind so it could grow kind
And less greedy and willfully blind

For us; all chance was gone.

As we were flowing into the other side
We tried to forget
What we could only regret.

III

We were expecting an open door
To a place better than we ever had before
But what we found was not as merry

As the place that we left behind.
We expected angels with wings
Singing in harmony

But we were met by birds of every Earthly kind;

Our bodies were broken
Beyond repair
But part of our minds

Went on living
And joined heaven's light;
Free from Negativity's plight;

DEATH RATTLE: Equity Lost included

Free from need;
No longer enslaved
In the Mastermind's greed.

IV

The Cold on the other side
Brought chills to the living too;
Shared thrills with those who knew

That we had returned
To our living Host
Earth and Sky

Never asking why
We were too ready to die
Before we really lived.

THE END

S. E. MCKENZIE

EQUITY
LOST

EQUITY LOST
I
Janis dressed for success
Walked by those who were dispossessed
Ignored those who would oppress

She built value through time.
Empowered;
She knew what was hers and what was mine.

She walked down the street
Lined with patio chairs;
Where many dined on lobster;

Many were owned by the Monster Mobster.

What was; sometime yesterday;
Will now fade away.
For today is a new day

The order of things
Beyond the upside down world
That could turn the glass ceiling into a floor

S. E. MCKENZIE

Safety net was gone
Angry Boys just like dots
Moving around on scatter plots

Janis hoped for a better life;
With her beau; even though
Monster Mobster

Held on to the Ghostly Boys; would not let them go.
So hurt inside
They wanted to hurt back somehow

Widening the Negative Zone
Where backpacks and everything they owned
Must be left at the door

Like getting kicked; felt so atrocious;
While they laughed; had to survive
Many became ferocious.

Obstruction everywhere; Ghostly Angry Boys
Lived in a world where no one could care
Broken spirits for evermore

No opening for engagement
Skateboards slamming
Into another door

DEATH RATTLE: Equity Lost included

Direction not so clear
Turning east they see
A steely beast

Turning west
They see the sea
Some say a doorway to Eternity

So how can it be
Necessary
To micromanage

Until their heart was broken
Life was never nothing at all
A long time ago

Life of quality
Depended on location of Equity.
What side are you on?

Behind the wall;
The winning side
Needs a losing side

No vision
When making a decision
Needed.

S. E. MCKENZIE

The micromanagers with guns
Were on watch all night
No one felt safe

Though we were told the process was right;
Would keep us safe;
Some felt too stifled and weak to speak.

The wall could not confine
Value
For it had a life of its own

As currency value paralleled oil
Prices in the bubble could only be inflated
Only machines were needed to toil

Before they became outdated
And what we said
Meant nothing at all

For we all were on the wrong side of the wall.

They had no words to speak
So the guns gave them might
While blood flowed

DEATH RATTLE: Equity Lost included

In us all night
Made us glad
To still be alive

Though we were told we were
Living in a world
Where goodness could not exist

And where we would never be missed;
As the youth were ran out of town;
The remaining few were always put down.

"My friends mean a lot
To me; too bad they were treated so bad,"
Janis almost said but left the thought inside her head.

The old felt the loss
And wondered why they were still so cross
While the future was being forced out of the door

The youth's world was turned upside down
The Glass Ceiling
Became the floor

S. E. MCKENZIE

Some of the youth hid under that floor
While the Monster Mobster laughed
As the old hid behind their fence of wire

Monster Mobster knew
Their fear
Would never tire.

And the old
Felt no sorrow
When the loss of their town's tomorrow

Was being pushed away
Not allowed to stay
Could not come back another day.

Now transient
The youth
Were only allowed a short stay

Though the cost of emergency shelter
Was more
Than a real home

DEATH RATTLE: Equity Lost included

Many went missing
And were under the ground.
They could not be found;

They made no sound;

The Monster Mobster
Kept on killing
For it was thrilling

And Janis knew
What it was like
To have nothing left to lose.

They held on to their energy
Within a rigid force
Frigid heart so cold

It got that way
As they grew old
Piling up their gold

Putting everyone down,
Always wearing a frown;
Whatever they did took too long.

S. E. MCKENZIE

They could not feel strong
For they were too tired
Confined behind their fence so wired.

During the time of yesterday
They had some things they desired
Hoping it would make them more admired

They had no clue
What would transpire
Behind that fence made of wire.

The Monster Mobster knew

When their pain had awoken
It would go unspoken
Even though they felt so broken.

The Monster Mobster took over the mind;
The Force was steely and very unkind
Made many willfully blind.

Scary city;
Used to be pretty;
Though there was no sorrow

DEATH RATTLE: Equity Lost included

When they locked out their tomorrow.
They needed no vision
To make a decision

For random luck
Was good enough
During the years gone by.

And the Dark Force was everywhere
Didn't care; treated everyone the same;
Even though the Dark Force didn't have a name.

For many; only escape was in drink;
Getting lost in the crowd;
When they awoke

The Ghostly Angry Boys
Were covered in ink
Still trapped in the poorest part of town

With no way out.

S. E. MCKENZIE

Called dangerous
Framed within
Self-fulfilling prophecies

Went on breaking
The heart
Before its awakening.

Their heartbeat was flattened
But not yet dead;
Heart had less intensity

To see the ever changing sky turn red.
One would have to ask why
Tomorrow was left forgotten.

And the ghosts of yesterday
Were flying in the wind;
We closed the window

And every curtain;
But the pain
Would still linger

DEATH RATTLE: Equity Lost included

Waiting to pound again.

Lost in the growing city
Rural fringe and all its Equity
Left hidden behind the fence of wire.

Give and take;
Anything less
A big mistake.

Equity;
What you learn
What you earn

What you return.

Steely Grandma watched
As Ghostly Angry Boys
Slammed their skateboards into glass.

In the Upside Down World

Monster Mobster was in charge of the Negative Zone
Where backpacks and everything you owned
Must be left outside the door;

S. E. MCKENZIE

It felt so atrocious;
To survive
One became ferocious.

Process of becoming transient
Was shadowed
Behind the new concrete and glitter.

And only a few felt sorrow
As they locked out their tomorrow
While counting their surplus

Of a little over a billion.
The pool contributors were 35 million;
Less than sixty dollars each;

They had nothing more to teach
And the future was out of reach.
For the transient walking in the halls

Between razor walls
Death; the other side of life.
Breath; you must take one

DEATH RATTLE: Equity Lost included

Even during times of strife.

Reality reflects
In the mirror of doom
And growing gloom;

In the poor part of town;
Just another Negative Zone.
Ghostly Angry Boys pick on those alone

Ghostly Angry Boys
With Steely Grandma
Who does not speak

But just drives them around
While the missing
Are sometimes under the ground

Never to be found
For they do not make a sound
They left their broken bodies

Behind; in a world where they were despised;

S. E. MCKENZIE

Never saying a word
As Ghostly Angry Boys
Slam their boards again;

Someone's Equity
In the Negative Zone
Had just been degraded

Couldn't sooth their pain
So Micromanaged
They did not know what to do

When their chain
Had been loosened
Had no principles

Just strange rituals
Made them feel
Like individuals.

II
Beautiful child
New to this world
There is so much he needs to know

DEATH RATTLE: Equity Lost included

Every day he will grow
Into a new tomorrow
There will be some sorrow

When he finds
Not everything thrown to the floor
Will bounce back up

Elasticity
By design
Up and down

Dead Cat in the hat
Bouncing off the wall
Before the fall.

Beautiful child
So new to this world
One day when he is old

He will have been told
To see nothing; hear nothing;
And serve with a smile

S. E. MCKENZIE

For he will only be here for a little while.

There will be lost years;
Trying to prove a negative
Time; well he would never have enough;

Even if the world managed;
To grow more love.
Trying to prove a negative

Would leave his psyche damaged;
Hurting too bad to smile
During his profile.

Which would try to define
A free spirit
Within a hard line.

Stay for only a short time;
Any longer it will be treated like a crime;
Hell; living in a world where you never belong.

III
Today is the day to take action
Can one fight evil to transform it
Or does fighting evil require evil deeds?

DEATH RATTLE: Equity Lost included

Bobby's son asked his father;
Who could not reply;
Felt dismay;

Did not know what to say;
"We all need someone to feed
Dying in all this greed,"

The father said as a reply
He did not want to lie;
Did not want his son to cry.

"So when you fight evil so atrocious;
To survive
One becomes ferocious."

"How do you know
If you are going to win?"
The son asked his dad

Hoping to not make him mad.
"I suppose you will never know"
As boy's dad remembered Ghostly Angry Boys

S. E. MCKENZIE

From a time, long ago.

"You might not survive
You could be buried alive
But the cause will never die

The cause will just grow
As it feeds from today's sorrow
Into tomorrow

And create a system
More brutal than he;
The one who will never see.

Manipulation through loss
Heartache grows into power
Becomes the boss."

The dad said as a reply
He did not want to lie
Did not want his son to cry.

"And this war will end all wars
That is what we are fighting for
A war to end all wars."

DEATH RATTLE: Equity Lost included

So atrocious;
To survive
One becomes ferocious.

The father added.
Sometimes though
If we see good in others

Our love can grow
So we become
Universal sisters and brothers.

After we see atrocity
It is harder
To be so free.

IV

"Modern War Machines
Costs how many houses?
How many trains?"

No one asked why
As they bowed down
To Carrot-stick god

S. E. MCKENZIE

And his War Machine.

Flown by a clone;
Wing man was a drone.
We were lost in this crowd

Felt so alone

Our minds no longer free;
First to go
Was Curiosity.

Many bowed down to Slander and Tyranny
Defining an enemy
Calmed the need to fear

Cultural conditioning
Economic Warfare
Where no one was rich enough

And where many despised the poor.
Cold faced;
She slammed the door;

Before anyone could ask for more.

DEATH RATTLE: Equity Lost included

And then she said,
"I don't need anyone to feed,
It is not my fault

They are dying in all this greed.
I am just influenced
By what I need.

It may seem atrocious;
To survive
One becomes ferocious.

V
Bow down
Show reverence
To your Carrot-stick god

Or drown
In the sea of blood
Now that the angel has emptied

His Bowl

S. E. MCKENZIE

To soothe his conscience
Neighbors will call him pious
No one will notice his bias

The numerator is zero
The denominator is zero
You get nothing from nothing

Rigid
One rule fits all
Before the fall

Leaves of color
Are still green
And the sun shines in our hair.

Lost elasticity
Diminished Equity
Loss of entitlement and citizenship

Zero was on top of Zero;
And nothing was made from nothing;
No longer a person of means;

DEATH RATTLE: Equity Lost included

For Equity was no longer seen alive in dreams.
Equity; more than just capital saved over the years;
Equity was about fairness in a world with so many tears.

As nothing from nothing grows.
The Crony Capitalist knows
The right people

While war machines delegate
Who to hate
Who to kill.

What a thrill;
To watch the machines
Fly inside the air

One way and wrong way
One dimensional
Is so intentional

Not really conventional
For innovation
Just is; without authorization

S. E. MCKENZIE

What didn't exist does now;
Without Documentation;
Just needed Consideration.

While refugees from the War Tone Zone
Know we can't care
And life is just not fair.

VI

Ghosts arrived in a swarm
Left their broken bodies behind
In a cold world often unkind

Fences of wire
Could never inspire
Left nothing to admire

The wind blew off a hat
The boy missed the bus
Before it turned

Exploded and burned
Unexpected;
Could not be predicted.

DEATH RATTLE: Equity Lost included

The losses were many
In the Divided City
Immortality

Was their only hope.

Modern War Machines
Fueled with dead matter and hard lines
Sometimes could not kill beyond the skin.

Many ran
Into a new life
So they could live new dreams

Forget the screams

As they followed
Living streams
Hope was kept alive

Only way to survive
As we; all refugees; of some sort;
Felt the sun

Shining on our hair.

S. E. MCKENZIE

Almost a prison land
Behind Mega Walls
And deleted border towns

The new Deceiver
Looked like a clown
With his upside down frown

To match the upside down world
Glass ceiling now a floor
Creating alienation throughout the nation.

Hate turned vibes into brick
Hate made many sick
Angry Ghostly Boys looking for someone to pick

A fight with; baiters and haters;

Only power they knew
Was making others crawl.
Otherwise they did nothing at all;

For Equity was no longer in dreams
And no one cared
Even though Equity was more

DEATH RATTLE: Equity Lost included

Than capital saved over the years
In a world
With way too many tears.

No one asked why
As they bowed down
To the Carrot-stick god

And His War Machine.

Flown by a clone;
Wing man was a drone.
We were lost in this crowd

And Janis felt so alone.

We all knew
More than ever before
Inequity was Tyranny's atrocity;

Made many look so atrocious.
And in order to survive
Many became ferocious.

It would take courage
To grow enough Goodwill and Love
To give Peace a chance.

THE END

S. E. MCKENZIE

Produced by S.E. McKenzie Productions
First Print Edition September 2015

DEATH RATTLE: Equity Lost included

Enquiries: 1(778)992-2453
Mailing Address:
S. E. McKenzie Productions
168 B 5th St.
Courtenay, BC
V9N 1J4

Email Address: messidartha@aol.com

http://www.amazon.com/SarahMcKenzie/e/B00H9RWX48
/ref=ntt_dp_epwbk_0

www.ingramcontent.com/pod-product-compliance
Lightning Source LLC
Chambersburg PA
CBHW060545030426
42337CB00021B/4443